D0045003

Meditation

Also by Brian L. Weiss, M.D.

*Healing the Mind and Spirit Cards
(available February 2003)

Many Lives, Many Masters

*Messages from the Masters:
Tapping into the Power of Love*

*Mirrors of Time: Using Regression for Physical,
Emotional, and Spiritual Healing*

Only Love Is Real: A Story of Soulmates Reunited

Through Time into Healing

Items with asterisks are available
through Hay House, Inc.:
(800) 654-5126 • www.hayhouse.com

Meditation

Achieving Inner Peace and Tranquility in Your Life

Brian L. Weiss, M.D.

Hay House, Inc.
Carlsbad, California • Sydney, Australia
Canada • Hong Kong • United Kingdom

Copyright © 2002 by Brian Weiss

Published and distributed in the United States by:
   Hay House, Inc., P.O. Box 5100, Carlsbad, CA 92018-5100
(800) 654-5126 • (800) 650-5115 (fax) • www.hayhouse.com
   Hay House Australia Pty Ltd., P.O. Box 515, Brighton-Le-Sands,
NSW 2216 • *phone:* 1800 023 516 • *e-mail:* info@hayhouse.com.au

Editorial supervision: Jill Kramer • *Design:* Ashley Parsons

**Cataloging-in-Publication Data
available from the Library of Congress**

ISBN 1-56170-930-1

05 04 03 02   4 3 2 1
1st printing, May 2002

Printed in the United States of America

Contents

Introduction

Over the past 20 years, I've come to be known for my work and research in the field of past-life therapy. Although this particular approach has helped many people, there are numerous paths that can be taken to attain inner growth and enlightenment. I've discovered that we have many dimensions to explore and enjoy, for our souls are endowed with possibilities far beyond the constraints of time and space. I believe that we're not simply human beings occasionally gifted with spiritual experiences, but instead, are spiritual beings who happen to undergo human experiences from time to time.

Meditation and Past-Life Therapy

In my first book, *Many Lives, Many Masters*, I wrote about how treating a woman named Catherine changed my life. Since I describe the experience in detail in that book, I'd like to just briefly touch on it here.

Catherine came to my office in 1980, suffering from anxiety, phobias, panic attacks, and troubled relationships. For 18 months, I treated her with traditional psychotherapeutic techniques, but since the signs of recovery were minimal, I decided to try hypnosis on her.

After inducing a trance, I asked her to go back to the time from which her symptoms arose. To my amazement, that suggestion took her back to a time approximately *4,000 years ago,* where she had originally suffered the traumatic experiences that were the root of her present-day problems. By recalling and reliving these incidents, she was then able to alleviate her symptoms.

But in addition to her memories, Catherine also brought back many messages from the Masters, who are highly evolved spirits whose wisdom and capacity for love enhance the spirituality of humankind. These messages moved me deeply and changed my view of the world, the way I saw my work, and my relationships with my patients. Before I met Catherine, my medical education had been rigorous and orthodox, and my psychiatric training had followed along traditional psychoanalytic lines; but after my experience with her, I began to explore alternative therapies that would help my patients. It was during this quest that I learned the value of meditation.

Many people like Catherine undergo traumatic experiences throughout their lifetimes that are so devastating that they can scar their minds and souls.

Some are indeed too painful to remain in their conscious memory. However, even if these memories are pushed down to the subconscious level, the experiences' effects still remain, together with residual physical and emotional reactions.

Just like hypnosis and other methods of past-life therapy, meditation progressively develops the ability to concentrate and to focus, thus gently tapping into the subconscious mind. Memories of past lives—and of the intervals in the spiritual state between these incarnations—are stored in the subconscious, which is the most creative and clairvoyant level of the mind. The subconscious is where we draw the spiritual resources that are so vital in our daily lives.

In my work with patients, I've noted that meditation enhances the ability to *remember*. In simple terms, what we do in past-life therapy is help people recall the origin of their symptoms, physical reactions, fears, rage, and pain. When the source of the trauma is finally located, people tend to let go of their symptoms, as they realize that the trauma is something that's already over, part of the past, and no longer a threat. I myself have had memories of my own past lives during deep meditation, as well as amazing insights that helped me solve problems in my current life. But not everybody needs this therapy, for not everyone suffers from hidden wounds or pain from past lives. There are other ways to achieve inner peace and balance while developing our spirituality—and chief among these is meditation. In fact, I've noticed that after my patients complete their past-life therapy, meditation helps consolidate their therapeutic gains.

In addition, I find it helpful for my patients to practice with a recording of one of my guided meditations during (and even after) their therapy, so I've included one on the CD that's packaged with this book, for you to listen to and enjoy.

What Is Meditation?

Meditation is the art or technique of quieting the mind so that the endless chatter that normally fills our consciousness is stilled. In the quiet of the silent mind, the meditator begins to become an observer, to reach a level of detachment, and eventually, to become aware of a higher state of consciousness.

The stresses of today's world seem to intrude constantly into our daily lives—even moments of relaxation and pleasure are curtailed as rising pressures and demands leave us bewildered. Under this barrage of stress, the physical body functions at a heightened level of alertness—the so-called fight-or-flight reaction—triggering a cascade of physiological reactions. Fear, a common complaint in today's world, also sets off internal alarms that urge us to act to protect ourselves. It's becoming more and more difficult to tune in to our inner selves, to remember our true spiritual nature.

Thankfully, the practice of meditation helps us

clear our minds. It rids us of stresses, intrusive thoughts, and fragments and echoes of the outside world—all of which disturb our conscious minds. Meditation makes our minds more sensitive to what's truly important. And the benefits extend well beyond the meditative state itself, although it's important to remember that meditation is in and of itself highly beneficial. The deeper that meditation takes us, the further we move away from the level of everyday consciousness (encompassing frustration, stress, anxiety, and worry), and the closer we draw to the higher self, with its capacity for love. Consequently, as we gain a higher perspective about life and our place in the world, appreciate the love that lies within us, and discover that we already possess this precious gift that's so full of beauty, we find ourselves filled with self-love and are able to achieve happiness and joy. We indeed become enlightened—and enlightening—beings.

Meditation demands practice and patience, but the act of meditating itself continues to generate more and more patience. After all, what's important is that you're getting reacquainted with the most beautiful, receptive, and productive part of yourself. There are many ways to contact this higher self of yours, and the more you progress along this path, the easier it becomes to achieve increasingly higher levels of spirituality. That's why in this book, I'll help you discover the techniques of meditation and visualization that will open your minds *and* your hearts.

Getting Started

It's easy to become entangled in problems and difficulties. You probably feel stuck at times, as if you just can't move forward in your life. But the solution may be as simple as setting aside just 20 minutes a day, every day, to meditate.

Start by sitting comfortably (or lying down if you prefer), closing your eyes, and just *relaxing*. Loosen your muscles and start to pay attention to your breathing, noticing any areas of tension. Send your body a message: *Everything is fine, everything is at peace. Relax, take it easy.* Ask each muscle to let go of tension and tightness.

Let scattered thoughts float gently out of your mind, and ask your mind to block out the clamoring voices that usually bombard you—one by one if necessary. Take one thing at a time, one problem at a time. Live *this* moment intensely—this precious, unique moment of grace, light, and elevation—by letting go and surrendering.

Because the present is the only place where you can find happiness and joy, psychospiritual therapy emphasizes mindfulness of the present moment. The human mind is a marvelous mystery, a creative masterpiece that can transport us either to the heights of joy or the depths of misery. Mindfulness is the awareness of those thoughts, emotions, feelings, and perceptions that are occupying us now. And so, by eliminating the distractions of the past and future, the act of meditating opens the door to inner peace and health. You can learn to focus on the present by concentrating on a single word, mantra, image, or sound—or by simply emptying your mind. (Listening to the meditation CD and focusing on its words will also help.)

By pulling us out of the rut of our everyday awareness, meditation serves as a reminder of what we've been learning about higher, more spiritual values. We're reminded of the bigger picture, of what's important to us in our lives and what isn't. Perhaps we'll become aware of a sudden understanding, a solution that hadn't previously occurred to us—or we might gain more clarity about a distressing situation, as though a light switch in a dark room was flipped on. This is what is called "insight," and it's how to awaken to ultimate reality.

Meditation As a Path to Love and New Beginnings

The capacity to love and feel loved restores balance. It sends us back into the world equipped with impressive skills. Since the subconscious is less sensitive to criticism and the judgments of others, it becomes a wellspring of creativity and intuition. Over time, continued contact with our authentic inner self empowers us to trust our own emotions and feelings and to realize the unique contribution that we make to the world.

Here's an example from my own life: At one point, my relationship with my son, Jordan, was rather thorny as we struggled through a rough patch of his adolescence. One day, while in a deep state of meditation, without any particular thoughts in my mind, I suddenly heard a booming voice inside my head. It was like a telepathic trumpet, and it shook my whole body.

"Just love him!" the voice thundered. I was instantly wide awake, for I knew the message was referring to Jordan.

One very early and dark morning a week later, I was driving Jordan to school. I tried to get a conversation going, but his responses were particularly monosyllabic that day. He was just plain grumpy.

I knew I had the choice of being angry or just letting

it go. I thought of the message—*Just love him!*—and I chose the latter.

"Jordan, just remember that I love you," I said as I dropped him off.

To my surprise, he replied, "I love you, too."

That was a great new start for us both.

In this book, I'll be using my experiences as a therapist to teach you about the benefits you may reap from meditation in at least three areas: (1) solving personal conflicts and difficult relationships; (2) helping the body and mind to heal; and (3) starting out on the path to spiritual growth and development. It's my hope that meditation will give *you* new beginnings, too.

Chapter One

Happiness Is

in the Present—

Using Meditation
to Overcome Conflicts

Ⓞne of the benefits of meditation is enhanced concentration. Ruminating on the past, or stockpiling fears about the future, is a waste of mental, emotional, and spiritual energy.

This squandering of energy makes me think of a typical business meeting, where people are greatly challenged by all of the tasks and tight deadlines involved in a project, and yet they can only think to bring up *more* difficulties by listing all of the things to be done in the future.

The pessimist in the group hints at horrifying scenarios: "No way! We won't make it . . . it's all too much!"

Then a clear-thinking voice will usually pipe up to say, "Well, we have to find a way to deal with this. Let's start with what absolutely needs to be done first, and *then* we'll see about the rest."

After this, discussions tend to become more productive, because when we manage to focus our thoughts and will on changing the present, the outcome is most often positive.

Seeing What's Right in Front of Us

I'd like to share an anecdote with you. Once I was teaching a patient of mine how to meditate. At the beginning of one of our sessions, she remarked, "I just saw the most beautiful tree!"

Intrigued, I asked, "Oh? Where did you see it?"

"In front of my house," she replied. It had always been there, but meditation had opened this woman's eyes to the beauty that had been within her reach—and that she'd neglected to see—every day. It just goes to show that when we learn to quiet our minds, we'll see the most beautiful things.

What happened to this patient and many others taught me a fundamental truth: *The past helps us learn from its lessons, and the future is for planning, but we live in the present—right here and right now.* This is where we can interact in both the outer world and within ourselves, where we can initiate change. Our spiritual development, and our joy, is always found in the present moment—which is where our actions are always anchored as well.

Here's another story that illustrates my point. Armando was a patient of mine who wasn't having any significant psychological or physical problems—yet he was very serious about seeking spiritual growth

3

and desperately wanted the experience of past-life regression.

Armando's personality bordered on the obsessive-compulsive. He had difficulty relaxing, and he preferred to spend his leisure time alone or with his wife rather than with other people. Although he was always polite and considerate, he wasn't overly giving or charitable toward others.

On our second session, I hypnotized Armando to a deep level. He experienced an ecstatic state, filled with peace and love. He also saw vivid colors, particularly purple, which is a deeply divine and regal color that's traditionally associated with spirituality. But even though he was trying very hard, he couldn't retrieve any past-life memories at all.

I gave Armando a tape with a relaxation exercise guided by my voice. His wife, whom I had never met, also listened to the tape. She, in turn, had vivid visualizations of several past-life scenes, and she recounted them to her envious husband. But Armando still saw nothing of his previous lifetimes.

However, on this same tape, I instruct the listener to try to meet a wise individual, guide, or helper. I then have the listener ask a question or two of this person, and pay attention to the answer. While listening to the tape, Armando again experienced the purple light, and out of this light, his guide materialized. His name was Michael, and he was a 19-year-old male with long blond hair who wore blue jeans and a plaid flannel shirt. With a big smile, Michael put his arm around Armando and told him, "Lighten up, relax, and don't be so serious."

The age, style, characteristics, and dress of this guide weren't what one would expect such a formal and uptight person as Armando to conjure up or imagine. Even Armando himself was surprised. Yet whenever Armando listened to the tape, Michael would emerge out of this purple light and talk to him. He imparted spiritual advice, helped with practical wisdom regarding Armando's business and personal relationships, and made several accurate predictions of events that came true almost immediately.

But Armando wasn't satisfied, for he still desperately wanted a past-life regression. As a result, he minimized the beauty and importance of the encounters with Michael, his guide.

During our third session, I hypnotized Armando to a deep level and had him find Michael.

"Ask *him* why you can't seem to remember your past lifetimes," I instructed.

Michael's answer was swift and to the point. "You will be allowed to remember your lifetimes as a reward when you give up your present fears. There is *nothing* to fear. You're afraid of people, and you shouldn't be. Don't worry about others—they'll be all right. Just don't expect them to be perfect. Go to them to help them, even if you begin with just one at a time."

It turns out that Armando, who was so focused on his past, didn't really need to remember other lifetimes, for his work was to be done in the here-and-now.

The practice of meditation can, and should, be focused on the present. On the one hand, we silence the disturbing voices that bind us to the past. On the other, we must block the often frightening pictures that we ourselves create to represent our concerns about the future. Since our own fears create these pictures, they're neither comforting nor pleasant—and since there are countless possible futures that we have available to us, these "pictures" may not necessarily manifest as the actual future.

Many of our personal conflicts and tensions can be resolved when meditation allows us to concentrate fully on the present. This is how we develop the ability to focus on what's important, minimizing extraneous thoughts. The practice of meditation needs persistence and tenacity, as negative thoughts may return repeatedly, often through mere force of habit.

Thich Nhat Hanh, the Vietnamese Buddhist monk and philosopher, uses the metaphor of enjoying a good cup of tea to illustrate mindfulness. You must be completely awake in the present to enjoy the tea, for only in the awareness of the present can your hands feel the pleasant warmth of the cup; only in the present can you savor the aroma, taste the sweetness, and appreciate the delicacy. If you're ruminating about the past or worrying about the future, you'll completely miss the experience of enjoying that cup of tea. You'll look down at the cup, and the tea will have vanished.

Life is like that: If you're not fully in the present, you'll look around and it will be gone. You'll have missed the feel, the aroma, the delicacy, and the beauty of life. It will seem to have sped past you.

The past is finished. Learn from it and let it go. As for the future, it isn't even here yet—of course you should plan for it, but don't waste your time worrying about it. *Worrying is worthless.* When you stop focusing on what has already happened and what may never happen, then you'll be in the present moment. *Then* you'll begin to experience joy in life.

In my own meditation, I once received a message that I found truly inspiring, which I'd like to share with you now:

8

With love and understanding comes the perspective of infinite patience. What's your hurry? There *is* no time anyway; it only feels that way to you. When you're not experiencing the present, when you're absorbed in the past or worried about the future, you bring great heartache and grief to yourself. Time is an illusion, too. Even in the three-dimensional world, the future is only a system of probabilities. Why do you worry so?

The past must be remembered and then forgotten. *Let it go.* This is true for childhood and past-life traumas; but it's also true for attitudes, misconceptions, and belief systems that have been drummed into you, and for all old thoughts—indeed, for *all* thoughts. How can you see freshly and clearly with those thoughts? What if you needed to learn something new, and with a fresh perspective?

Stop thinking. Instead, use your intuitive wisdom to experience love again. Meditate. See that everything is interconnected. See your true self. See God.

Meditation and visualization will help you stop thinking so much and will help you begin the journey back. Healing will occur. You will begin to use your unused mind. You will see. You will understand. And you will grow wise. Then there will be peace.

The wisdom of those words seems to be reflected in the story I heard from a rather remarkable man while I was on a trip to South America. Eduardo had been a political activist in the 1970s, and he had been wanted by the police. In order to avoid prison, he fled to a remote spot deep in the heart of his country, where he lived in a simple house that was surrounded by heavily wooded mountains.

"I used to spend hours sitting by the window, as there was nothing else for me to do," Eduardo told me. "All the time I wondered about what was happening in the towns and in the nation as a whole. I had a sense of oppression deep inside, and I felt hunted, like the world was closing in around me. It was hell at first. But little by little, these things began to fade into the distance. I don't know how long it took, maybe a week or so. I started to spend my time just gazing out at the forest, looking at the bushes, the trees, and the mountains. Outside, it looked like an endless sea of rolling hills, stretching as far as my eyes could see. . . .

"One day, I realized that all of those people on my

trail would never be able to find me—no matter how powerful they were—if I hid myself behind one of the bushes on top of those mountains. It seemed like a dumb idea, but it calmed me down quite incredibly and helped me through those days. And I started to enjoy sitting by that window and looking at all of that greenery. It was a beautiful forest out there, a really magnificent view."

Eduardo had intuitively developed a way of meditating. He was virtually hypnotized by the landscape around him, and as his tensions eased, he was able to be more alive and receptive in the present moment. Consequently, he was able to become aware of all of the subtleties and enchantment of nature. Seen from a fresh standpoint, his situation seemed less threatening, and with this new approach, he was able to consider a way out.

Our own resentments, hates, frustrations, and obsessions can be transformed by the same process. Meditation offers us a chance to escape from our physical selves. Viewed from a higher perspective, our problems fade. True healing and balance depend on reencountering our spiritual essence.

Turning on the Light Inside

Sometimes, simple acts of kindness can pierce the heart of a problem and heal relationships at a deep level much more profoundly than intellectual approaches can. This may require transcending the personal ego and pride, and letting go of the need to be "right."

One time, a visibly upset woman approached me and said, "I really feel terrible when I look back at the strict, authoritarian way I brought up my eldest son when he was little. I was very young and immature, and I simply raised him the way my mother raised me. I wish I could start over!"

I replied, "Love him *now* the way you wish you had when he was a child."

A year later, I met this woman again. She was

pleased with the progress she had made, for regular meditation had helped her break away from the effective paralysis her guilt had imposed on her. The end result was that she was able to draw closer to her son, as she showered on him all of the love and attention that had backed up within her.

It's amazing how the insights provided by meditating can transport even difficult personal relationships into a broader perspective. It's as if a light within us turns on, helping us to understand the other person more fully. Or perhaps it helps us prioritize what's important in the relationship and what isn't. Whatever the reason, empathy and compassion are great healers.

For someone with limited understanding, even small things can seem like the end of the world. But for a soul aware of its vastness, solutions are easier. The soul is never trapped or hopeless, for life is too important to submit to unhappiness and despair.

Chapter Two

Directing Our

Inner Light—

Using Meditation to Heal
Our Bodies and Minds

Many physicians know that people have curative energies within them that can play a decisive role in fighting disease. As some of my patients who were suffering from very serious illnesses taught me, this healing energy may be quite subtle, but it's incredibly powerful.

Frances, a patient of mine in her mid-40s, came to me to work on some relationship issues; she had also just been diagnosed as having two suspicious lumps in her right breast. Having set an appointment for surgery the Monday after our appointment, she was naturally quite nervous. So, during our session, I guided her in a meditation in which I had her visualize light entering and healing her body. I also gave her an audiotape containing a relaxation and healing meditation, and I suggested that she repeat this exercise at home. Frances agreed to do so.

The following Monday, Frances went to the hospital for the surgery. As part of the preparation for the procedure, her radiologist ran a final x-ray and mammogram—but to the surprise of the surgical team, they were unable to find the lumps that had been present on her previous workup. While Frances was on the operating table, the doctors argued over how to proceed. As he studied the x-rays, the surgeon refused to believe his own eyes and was determined to operate. However, the radiologist, who was highly respected by his peers, insisted that the lumps had disappeared.

Finally, Frances took matters into her own hands. "There aren't any lumps there," she said. "I'm going home." And she did.

Later, I received a note from Frances that said, "Thank you for the meditation regression tape. I'm 'living proof' that the healing light works!"

I'm quite convinced that we can *all* tap into the healing powers that lie within each and every one of us. Perhaps this is true holistic medicine, where we mobilize the *entire* organism, including the mind and the spirit.

For example, in his excellent book *Head First: The Biology of Hope and the Healing Power of the Human Spirit*, Norman Cousins carefully documented work that has helped to develop the new area of medical research known as *psychoneuroimmunology*—the study of how emotions affect the immune system. In addition, researchers at Harvard University have found that some types of meditation can prolong life in the elderly.

In a study reported in *The Lancet* (the prestigious British medical journal), medical researchers found that a combination of diet, exercise, and the practice of stress-reduction techniques can actually *reverse* blockages in coronary artery disease. Changes in diet and exercise alone won't do it—stress reduction was a necessary factor, far more important than physicians had originally believed.

As Dr. Dean Ornish, the coordinator of the study, commented, "This finding suggests that conventional recommendations . . . may be enough to prevent heart disease, but not to reverse it."

Relaxation, visualization, meditation, and regression can be used in order to eliminate stress, tension, fears, and phobias in a holistic way. I teach my patients meditation techniques that they can immediately incorporate into their daily routines, as well as use for the rest of their lives. These techniques can reduce insomnia, for instance, as well as help with

18

weight control, smoking cessation, stress reduction, strengthening the immune system, fighting infections and chronic illness, and lowering blood pressure. The health ramifications seem endless. I'm quite convinced that regular meditation is a priceless tool for the recovery and maintenance of health, for the chemistry and the physics of the body are indeed influenced by mental and spiritual energies. This is a new context for rethinking health care, and for utilizing practices that release these curative energies.

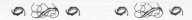

Chapter Three

Gateway to the

Eternal Dimension—

Using Meditation
As an Initiation to
Spiritual Development

Meditation can open up possibilities for spiritual experiences, almost as if the subconscious mind is itself the gateway to the eternal dimension. This gateway is never wide open, and there usually aren't any signs above it advising us where the road will lead at any given moment. Opening this gate isn't merely a matter of finding a key or saying some magic word—it's more like the idea that guided the ancient alchemists: the process of transforming and being transformed. Another way of looking at it is to say that the mind becomes a passage, and the person meditating turns into an individual who's able to recognize the passage and move through it into deeper, more transcendent states.

At times, this path we're on might bring us to a heightened awareness of our spiritual essence and to a state of profound ecstasy, lightness, satisfaction, and well-being, which represent contact with our deepest dimension. It may spread through us when we're contemplating something that gives us pleasure, or it may be intermittent, brief, and somewhat unspectacular. No matter the duration, the effect is the same: Heightened spiritual awareness glows on enlightened faces, reflecting joy and serenity.

One sure characteristic of spiritual illumination is that the person experiencing it radiates compassion and love to others without expecting anything in return. The enlightened person feels a oneness with every other person and being, with all there is. For instance, you can often see this effect in children at play or in people in love, for such individuals are directly experiencing the joy of the altered state. I've also witnessed this in some of my patients who have gained transcendent insights during a particularly powerful therapy session.

The many ways of achieving this feeling, or of letting oneself be touched by it, quite naturally vary from person to person. And although I've gained much knowledge and wisdom through my patients, I feel that it's been necessary for me to develop my own channels to receive this heightened awareness. For example, meditation has helped me receive messages, transcendent thoughts, intuition . . . and it's also helped me encounter my own past lives.

Somewhere in Time...

My first experience with a vivid past-life recollection came to me when I went to an acupressure (shiatsu) therapist because of chronic back and neck pain. The sessions were conducted in silence, and I used this quiet time to meditate. About an hour into my third session, I had reached a very deep state of relaxation when I was startled by a crystal-clear image of myself from another time.

In this scene, I was taller and thinner, with a small dark pointed beard, and I was wearing a multicolored robe. I realized that I was a priest, an extremely powerful member of the religious hierarchy of the time. The building in which I found myself had a strange design that I had never seen before. It was distinctly geometric—flat on top with a larger, wide bottom and sloping sides. There were seven or eight levels, with plants growing on and over the sides, and wide stairs connecting the levels at certain points. Gradually, I became aware of a word in my mind: *ziggurat.* I had no idea what this word meant, and decided to put it out of my mind for the time being.

While I flipped back and forth between the outlook and vision of the priest and to an outside, detached, overall perspective, I became intimately aware of this person's life. I knew that the priest's earlier idealism and spirituality had given way to material values as he ascended to a position of great power and authority—he even had the ear of the royal family. But instead of using his position to promote spiritual values, brotherhood, and peacefulness in his people, he abused his position to obtain wealth, sex, and even more power.

The priest died a very old man, and never recaptured the virtues and idealism of his youth. He had to leave behind his fortune, power, position, and body, all of which he had been so obsessed with. I felt a terrible sadness, for it seemed to me that this man had wasted his life.

Later that evening, I remembered the word *ziggurat.* I researched it in the encyclopedia and found out that a ziggurat is a temple of the same geometric shape that I had visualized. These temples originated from the Babylonian-Assyrian era, and the Hanging Gardens of Babylon is an example of such a structure. In this way, I was able to help narrow down the time period of my past life.

Ultimately, becoming aware of the priest's experiences induced a transient sadness in me, since he had squandered his opportunities for teaching about love and compassion. Experiences such as these can provide explanations (or at least clues) to why we run into certain situations and opportunities in our current lives—it's as though the spiritual lessons we encountered in the past are still there for us to learn from today.

Most of my patients are able to recall past lives during actual regression therapy. However, the regular practice of meditation may lead to past-life memories as well. This is because the constant practice of

26

meditation takes us to increasingly deeper levels of our inner selves. If you should find yourself experiencing past-life memories, don't try to determine if they're actual recollections or if they're metaphors, symbols, or simply products of your imagination. Just go with it. If you're uncomfortable, simply open your eyes and end the meditation. Exploring past lives through meditation is actually quite safe, because the unconscious mind is very wise and won't let anything harmful move through to your memory.

Other Spiritual Benefits of Meditation

The possibility of spiritual development offered by meditation isn't limited to revisiting past lives. In fact, some of my patients have undergone the experience of seeming to detach from their physical bodies during meditation. It's as if they float above the place where their body is, and they watch themselves. This is called an *out-of-body experience* (OBE). An OBE is important because it's a demonstration that there's more to "life" than what the physical body and the brain experience. An OBE is not at all dangerous, because the person will always be able to safely find their way back to their body.

An OBE is quite similar to what people who have undergone a *near-death experience* (NDE) describe. In these situations, usually due to illness or trauma, consciousness detaches from the physical body, and some people become aware of a brilliant light that seems to have tremendous spiritual significance for them. However, the person having the NDE quickly finds out that it's not yet time for them to die, and they soon return to their bodies.

Intuition is another type of spiritual experience that regular meditation enhances. It's almost as if knowledge, wisdom, and other significant revelations are whispered to our consciousness by an inner voice, and the more we open ourselves to this intuitional wisdom, the clearer the message becomes. It's important to learn to listen to this voice and trust its guidance. Personally speaking, I find that my strongest thoughts, images, and ideas often come to me when I'm deeply relaxed or meditating. I often remember the words a Master once said to me: *"The intellect is important in the three-dimensional world, but intuition is even more crucial."*

∾ ❦ ∾

Meditation can also open us up to receive messages from people in other dimensions. Following is an example of this.

Several years ago, I conducted a two-day seminar in Puerto Rico, which was attended by nearly 500 people. Many individuals experienced early childhood, in-utero, and past-life memories. One participant, a highly re-garded forensic psychiatrist, experienced even more.

During a guided meditation on the second day of the conference, his inner eye perceived the shadowy figure of a young woman, who approached him and said, "Tell them I am well. Tell them Natasha is well."

As he related his experience to the group, the psychiatrist said he felt "very silly." After all, he didn't know anybody named Natasha—the name itself is a rarity in Puerto Rico. And the message related by the ghostlike girl had no connection to anything happening in the conference or in his personal life.

"Does this message have any meaning to anybody here?" the puzzled psychiatrist asked the audience.

Suddenly, from the back of the auditorium, a woman screamed: "My daughter, my daughter!"

This woman's daughter was a young lady in her early 20s who had died suddenly only six months previously. The young woman's name was Ana Natalia, but her mother—and only her mother—called her "Natasha."

The psychiatrist had never met or even heard of Natasha or her mother, and was as unnerved by this extraordinary experience as the mother was. When both had regained their composure, Natasha's mother showed him a photo of her daughter. The psychiatrist grew pale, for this was indeed the same young woman whose spectral figure had approached him with her amazing message.

In Conclusion

I want to encourage you to meditate so that you, too, can discover and develop spiritual experiences— but remember to keep your mind open to whatever may occur. The experiences may take the form of feelings, images, memories of this life or of past lives, intuitional advice and wisdom, or even more transcendent states. Remember that there's a reason and a meaning for everything in your life—for living, for re-living, for each existence that you've had, for the gift

31

of recalling that existence. There's always a higher plan or project under way . . . or, at the very least, an opportunity for you to learn. Finally, don't forget that all of this tends to take time and practice, so be patient with the process and yourself.

ⓐ🖎ⓐ   ⓐ🖎ⓐ

Chapter Four

Magnificence

Waits for Us—

Using Meditation
to Know Ourselves

Although there are many things that I cannot yet explain—and I don't know if I'll *ever* be able to explain them—I do know that regular meditation can help us discover our most powerful and essential selves.

Although this path requires persistence and dedication, it demands far less of us than the storms and traumas of our daily lives. And even though it's a solitary journey, it's one that allows us to discover that we're really never alone. Therefore, the practice of meditation takes on added significance.

Meditation isn't merely a means to attain enlightenment; it's also an extremely worthwhile process in and of itself, for it helps us get in touch with our true selves. Getting to know ourselves is the best way to learn, for this is how we can ultimately transform our fears and limitations into power and joy.

The main lesson to be learned in life is to love other people—and ourselves—unconditionally. This is the knowledge that makes us divine, and it's the essence of meditation. Every step you take is sacred; every breath you breathe is holy. If you understand and practice these lessons, you'll be mindful, and your consciousness will shift from the everyday to the "other" perspective. You'll become observant, detached, and free from judgment.

Here are some vitally important things for you to re-member.

- You are greater than your body and greater than your mind.

- You are a marvelous being of light and love, immortal and eternal.

- You are greater than your fears, anxieties, bitter-ness, and worries—you are even greater than your own suffering.

- You are *always* surrounded by love—a love that can protect, comfort, and nourish you and offer you fulfillment. And you can directly experience the love surrounding you at any time. You can reencounter it in the depths of your own being, in your inner immensity, from where you have always managed to gaze out at the world—realizing, on some level, that you can make it a happier place for your-self and for others.

Close your eyes. Relax. Breathe. Concentrate. Imagine or visualize yourself wrapped in a beautiful spiritual light, absorbing this light and also radiating it out to your loved ones. Feel the tension and heaviness leaving your body, as though a great weight has been lifted from your shoulders. Focus your mind on the light. You are ready to begin the journey within.

A magnificent universe awaits.

Chapter Five

A Final Word—

Help with Meditation

As I became increasingly aware of the important role that meditation plays in spiritual growth, peace, and happiness, I began to recommend it to my patients and workshop participants. However, many of them told me that they found it difficult to concentrate and could meditate more easily if they had access to instructions and guidance such as the ones I offered them during individual sessions and workshops. I decided to record the guided meditation CD included in this book to answer these requests. I want to do as much as I can to help people perfect this practice, which is so crucial to our physical, emotional, and spiritual balance.

I know that the frantic pace of life can make you feel as if you don't have time to slow down and meditate, but it's important that you *make the time* for this investment in yourself. Commitment to the meditative process can rid the mind of those countless inconsequential thoughts that distract you on a daily basis.

Set aside 20 minutes for meditation every day if possible; you'll soon realize that it becomes easier and easier to find the time as you start to reap the benefits. Some of my patients enjoyed rich and significant experiences the very first time they used the CD, while others needed more practice. Even I had to meditate daily for three months before I was able to attain a stronger awareness. Just remember to be patient, and try not to get frustrated as you go along—for in order to reach increasingly deeper levels, it's important to meditate *regularly.*

A common misconception is that you must contort yourself into the lotus position in order to practice meditation—this really isn't necessary. You can meditate while lying down, sitting, or reclining comfortably. The goal is to relax, stop thinking, observe and detach, and become mindful and aware.

୭ ⬯ ୭

Let's get started. First, put on some comfortable, loose clothing, and pick a quiet place where you won't be interrupted. Try to free your mind from expectations, remaining open to all possibilities. If at *any time* you become uncomfortable with the process, simply open your eyes and end the exercise.

Understand that when you're meditating, you never

give up control to someone else. No "forces" take over your mind or body, nor do you enter a "time machine." You'll merely be concentrating very deeply, and know that you'll be in no danger whatsoever. In the meditative state, you can be inspired, touch higher levels of awareness, or be reawakened to your divine nature. These are pathways to enlightenment.

This CD is a powerful, life-changing tool for growth, but it isn't intended to be a substitute for medical care. If you're dealing with any significant mental or emotional disorder, are undergoing psychotherapy, are experiencing seizures, or have any neurological illness, I suggest that you consult your physician or therapist first and only use the CD under their supervision.

Remember: *Do not use this CD while driving or operating machinery or equipment that requires your attention and concentration.*

I sincerely hope that you enjoy these exercises and that they will help to bring you peace and harmony and will foster your spiritual growth.

Meditation CD: Transcript

At first, focus on your breathing, your breath. Let it be nice and deep and even . . . relaxed yoga breathing. This is the way within. With each breath, let yourself go deeper and deeper and deeper into a relaxed, serene, tranquil state. This is so healthy for your mind and for your body . . . to relax . . . to go within . . . to feel the peace.

With each breath, deeper and deeper . . . relaxed, peaceful, and calm. As you do this, relax all of your muscles. Your facial muscles and jaw . . . the muscles of your neck and shoulders . . . completely relaxing. The muscles of your back, both upper back and lower back. And of your arms. And the muscles of your stomach so that your breathing stays deep and even, relaxed, and serene. And lastly, the muscles of your legs. Completely relaxing your whole body now. Going deeper and deeper, feeling lighter . . . a serene and beautiful state. . . .

Your breathing stays nice and deep . . . relaxed and peaceful . . . all of your muscles relaxing. You can feel the calm. Let yourself go even deeper. . . .

Next, visualize or imagine a beautiful light coming in through the top of your head . . . and beginning to spread down your body, from above to below. A beautiful, powerful, healing light. You choose the color or colors. This light is connected with the light above and around . . . the divine light . . . a powerful light . . . a healing light because it heals every cell, every fiber, every tissue, every organ of your body . . . restoring all of these cells to the normal healthy state. Getting rid of illness . . . getting rid of disease . . . getting rid of discomfort . . . restoring to perfect health. This is a deepening light because it will bring you to a deep level of peace and relaxation. . . .

Allow yourself to go even deeper now . . . even deeper. . . .

And the light spreads down and fills all of the cells, the tissues in your face, in the back of your head. It flows gently into your neck, soothing and relaxing the muscles of the neck. The spinal cord . . . and your throat, it smooths the lining of your throat. And you go even deeper. It flows into your shoulders and down your arms . . . healing and relaxing every muscle and nerve, every fiber and every cell of your body as it reaches your hands. And you go even deeper. . . .

And it flows in to your heart, releasing the beautiful energy that is stored there. Healing your heart, filling your lungs, which glow beautifully in the light. And you go even deeper. Now you are feeling so peaceful,

47

so relaxed. Deeper and deeper with each breath. . . .

And the light flows into your back . . . healing and relaxing the large muscles and nerves. And it flows into your stomach and abdomen, filling up all of the abdominal organs and healing them as well. Relaxing the nerves and the muscles of the abdomen. Flowing past your hips now and down both legs, this beautiful, healing, soothing, deepening light—reaching to your feet. Filling your body now, and you feel so peaceful, so relaxed, so serene and calm. Let yourself go even deeper. . . .

You will be able to focus on my voice, but let other noises, thoughts, or distractions only deepen your level even more as they fade away. . . .

Next, visualize or imagine the light completely surrounding the outside of your body as well, as if you were in a halo or a bubble of light. And this protects you. No harm can come through the light, only goodness.

And it heals your skin and your outer muscles and deepens your level even more. . . .

In a few moments, I am going to count backwards from ten to one. With each number, let yourself go even deeper. So deep that by the time I reach one, your mind is no longer limited by the usual barriers of space or of time. So deep that you can experience all levels of your multidimensional self. So deep that you can remember everything. Every experience you have ever had. You can remember everything.

Ten . . . nine . . . eight . . . going deeper and deeper with each number back . . . seven . . . six . . . five . . . deeper and deeper and deeper . . . four . . . three . . . very, very deep. So peaceful, so calm and relaxed . . . two . . . nearly there . . . one . . . good!

In this beautiful, relaxed, serene state, imagine yourself, visualize yourself walking down a beautiful staircase. Down, down . . . deeper and deeper . . . down,

down. Each step down, increasing the depth of your level even more. . . . And as you reach the bottom of the stairs, in front of you is a beautiful garden. A garden filled with flowers, trees, grass, benches and places to rest, fountains. A beautiful place . . . safe, serene. And you go into this garden. Visualize yourself in the garden now. And here your body can completely rest and continue to heal itself, still filled with the wonderful light. As you go deeper and deeper . . . your body will refresh, renew, rejuvenate, recuperate . . . continuing to heal and fill with the beautiful energy so that later on after you are awake, you will feel wonderful, filled with the beautiful energy, refreshed, renewed, and yet in full control of your body and your mind. . . .

As your body rests and relaxes in the garden and fills with the beautiful energy . . . this is a time for healing, for relaxing, for finding that deep and beautiful peace within . . . for letting go of all tensions and all anxieties . . . for repairing . . . for letting go of the world and all of its troubles. . . . Going deep, deep within . . . to let go

50

of fear . . . and tension. . . . Let go of all negative thoughts and emotions. . . . Let go of fear, there is nothing for you to fear. Let go of tension, worry, anxiety. Let go of anger . . . and frustration. . . . Let go of sadness and grief and despair. Instead, fill yourself with peace and love and joy and bliss. This is your true inner state. And as your body rests and repairs and recuperates and refreshes, let the deepest, deepest parts of your mind . . . of your spirit . . . also refresh . . . and heal . . . and find the deep peace which lies within. . . .

You are a beautiful and wonderful being. Immortal, eternal . . . existing beyond all limits, beyond your body and beyond your mind . . . a being of eternal peace and love and bliss. As you feel this, continue to let go of fear . . . to let go of anxiety and of sadness . . . and of all other negative thoughts and emotions. Just feel the peace, and go deeper and deeper. . . . You may be immersed in colors. This will be healing, as well as relaxing. You may sense this. You may feel others around you. . . . You are never alone. You are always protected. . . .

Staying very, very deep . . . the healing relaxation envelops you, surrounds you . . . as you stay in the garden. . . . You have nowhere else to go now, nothing to do . . . no one to bother you. . . . Just to rest, to relax, to go deeply within, to feel the peace, the love, the joy of this inner state . . . to recuperate and repair, to fill yourself with light and love. . . .

In the ancient meditations, there is one . . . which is a love meditation. It teaches you to fill yourself with love. That feeling which can bring a tear of joy to your eye . . . fill yourself with it . . . feel this joy. In love, all fear dissolves. There is no fear. . . .

Visualize now, yourself, throughout all of your ages. From childhood, when you were a joyful, alive, vibrant, wonderful child . . . through the growing-up years . . . to your current age. . . . And surround yourself in this beautiful light. . . . You of all ages . . . this is all of you, there is no time. . . . You are safe. You are surrounded in light. Send yourself this light, this love.

And bring all of these images of you into your heart . . . so that you are complete. And there is nothing to fear. You are safe. . . .

And now, visualize or imagine your loved ones. And you can send them light and love as well. Surround them in light. Let them know how much you love. . . .

And this light protects, and it heals . . . and it connects you always . . . and whoever needs your light, your love . . . you can beam them . . . directly . . . now. . . . And bring them into your heart as well. . . .

And now, as you are filled with light and surrounded . . . and completely relaxed and serene and calm and peaceful . . . imagine that a wise and loving being comes to join you in the garden. . . . And you can communicate with this being . . . whether through words or symbols or images or thoughts or feelings. It doesn't matter. You can ask a question . . . and listen for the answer. . . . You can ask for what you need . . . . Whether this is a guide, a friend, a reflection of your higher self or something different, it does not matter. . . . Listen for the wisdom . . . feel the peace and the love. . . .

In love, there is no fear, no anxiety, no time, and no space. It is absolute. . . .

And as you love yourself, you give up all negativity. Not just thoughts which are negative and feelings which are harmful, but also habits and behaviors that do not promote love and well-being and peace. . . .

Giving up all harmful behavior because you do not need these anymore . . . listen for the answers . . . whenever you need this communication . . . you can be there. If it is safe to close your eyes, to go deeply within, just take a few deep breaths. Fill yourself with light. Put yourself back in the garden and you will be there. . . .

If you are in a situation where you cannot close your eyes . . . just take a few deep breaths. Immediately, you will feel the peace, the relaxation, the serenity. And even though you stay in complete control, alert, awake, in full control of your body and mind, you will still be filled with peace and understanding, calmer, and more joyful than before. . . .

And now, it is time to awaken. And I will awaken you by counting up from one to ten. . . . With each number, you'll be more and more awake and alert, in full control of your body and your mind. Feeling wonderful. Feeling great, refreshed, relaxed, and yet filled with a beautiful energy.

One . . . two . . . three . . . gradually awakening, feeling wonderful . . . four . . . five . . . six . . . more and more awake and alert. Feeling great . . . seven . . . eight . . . nearly awake now . . . nine . . . ten.

About the Author

Brian L. Weiss, M.D., maintains a private practice in Miami, Florida, where his offices include well-trained and highly experienced psychologists and social workers who also use regression therapy and the techniques of spiritual psychotherapy in their work. In addition, Dr. Weiss conducts seminars and experiential workshops nationally and internationally, as well as training programs for professionals.

Other meditation and regression audiotapes and CDs are available. For more information, please contact:

The Weiss Institute
6701 Sunset Drive, Suite 201 • Miami, FL 33143
Phone: (305) 661-6610 • Fax: (305) 661-5311
e-mail: in2healing@aol.com
www.brianweiss.com

(The exercise on this CD was previously available through The Weiss Institute as *Meditation to Inner Peace, Love, and Joy.*)

Other Hay House Titles
of Related Interest

Books

Chakra Clearing, by Doreen Virtue, Ph.D.

Infinite Self, by Stuart Wilde

Meditations, by Sylvia Browne

The Reconnection: Heal Others, Heal Yourself,
by Dr. Eric Pearl

You Can Heal Your Life Companion Book,
by Louise L. Hay

Audio Programs

Intuitive Healing: Five Steps to Developing Intuition,
by Judith Orloff, M.D.

Journeys into Past Lives, by Denise Linn

Karma Releasing, by Doreen Virtue, Ph.D.

Reversing Heart Disease: The Nonsurgical Approach,
by Julian Whitaker, M.D.

Sylvia Browne's Tools for Life, by Sylvia Browne

Your Journey to Enlightenment,
by Dr. Wayne W. Dyer

Card Decks

The Four Agreements Cards, by DON Miguel Ruiz

Healing with the Angels Oracle Cards,
by Doreen Virtue, Ph.D.

Inner Peace Cards, by Dr. Wayne W. Dyer

Zen Cards, by Daniel Levin

All of the above are available
at your local bookstore,
or may be ordered
through Hay House, Inc.

We hope you enjoyed this Hay House book.
If you would like to receive a free catalog featuring
additional Hay House books and products,
or if you would like information about the
Hay Foundation, please contact:

Hay House, Inc.
P.O. Box 5100, Carlsbad, CA 92018-5100

(760) 431-7695 or **(800) 654-5126**
(760) 431-6948 (fax) or **(800) 650-5115 (fax)**

Hay House Australia Pty Ltd
P.O. Box 515, Brighton-Le-Sands, NSW 2216
phone: 1800 023 516 • *e-mail:* info@hayhouse.com.au

Please visit the Hay House Website at:
www.hayhouse.com